Boy Soup
or
When Giant Caught Cold

Loris Lesynski
Illustrated by Jane Wallace-Mitchell

CELEBRATION PRESS
Pearson Learning Group

Giant woke up with a big, hurting head.
"I am sore, I am sick, I feel awful," he said.
He coughed—
moving mountains.
He hacked—
causing quakes.
He said, with a whimper,
"My everything aches."
Groaning, he shoved his blankets aside,
and reached for his *Giants' Home Medical Guide*.

With sofa-sized fingers,
he leafed through the book,
and in between sneezes
so loud that he shook,
he found all his symptoms—
page seventy-one:
"Queasiness,
wheeziness,
coughing begun.
Completely depleted,
and tending to droop."

The only prescription?

A bowl of
Boy Soup.

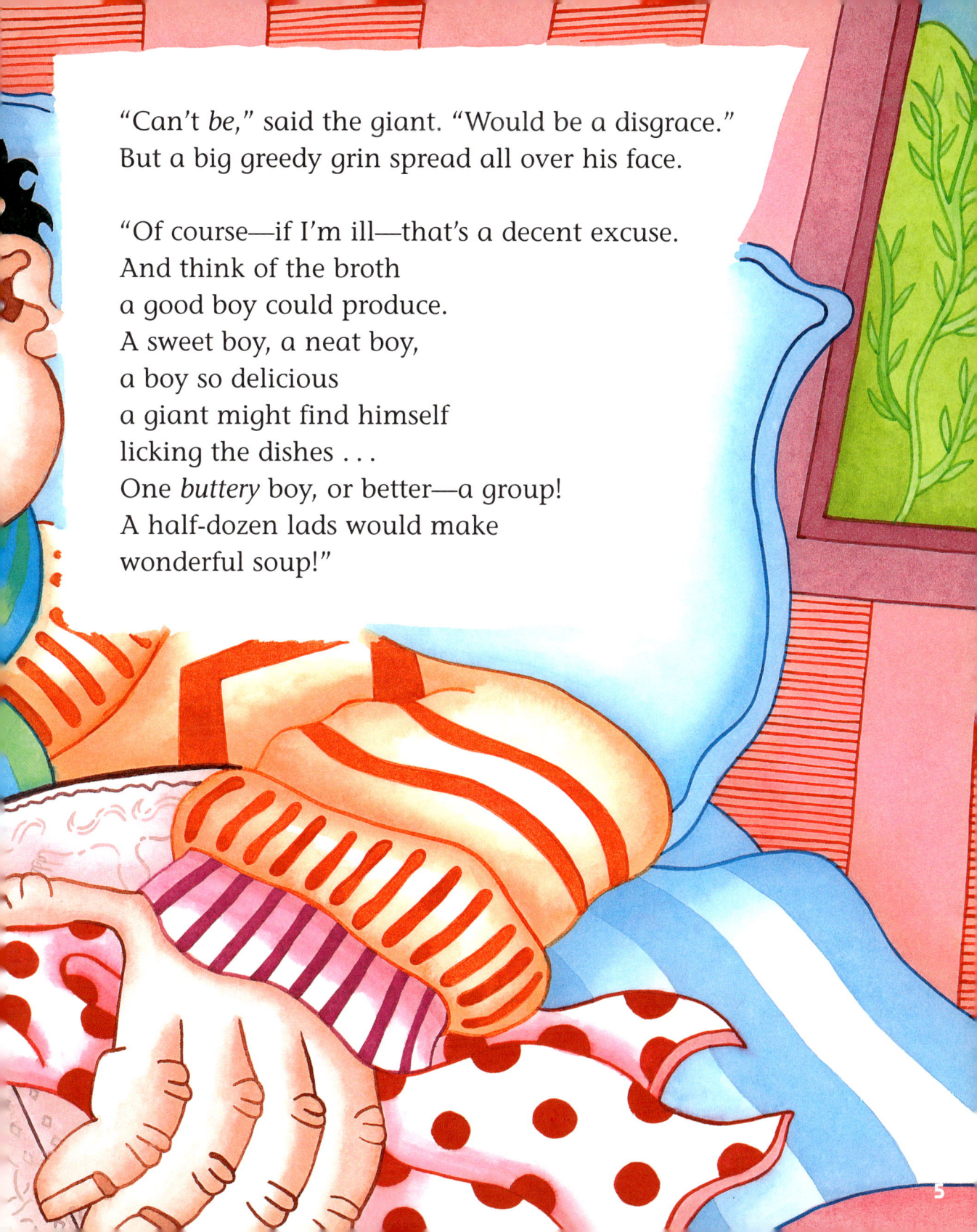

"Can't *be*," said the giant. "Would be a disgrace."
But a big greedy grin spread all over his face.

"Of course—if I'm ill—that's a decent excuse.
And think of the broth
a good boy could produce.
A sweet boy, a neat boy,
a boy so delicious
a giant might find himself
licking the dishes . . .
One *buttery* boy, or better—a group!
A half-dozen lads would make
wonderful soup!"

Catching the boys was as easy as pie.
He stretched down his thick giant
arm through the sky
and rested his hand at the top of a tree
where children were playing.
They just didn't see—
the branch they were grabbing
could grab *them*.
Too late!
That's how the giant got five boys—
and Kate.

"Why *should* I feel guilty—"
the giant began,
when six angry children
protested his plan.

"It's here in this
authorized medical book!"

Kate asked, "Before supper,
could *I* have a look?"

She read every word in the faded ink and said, "May I have just a minute to think?"

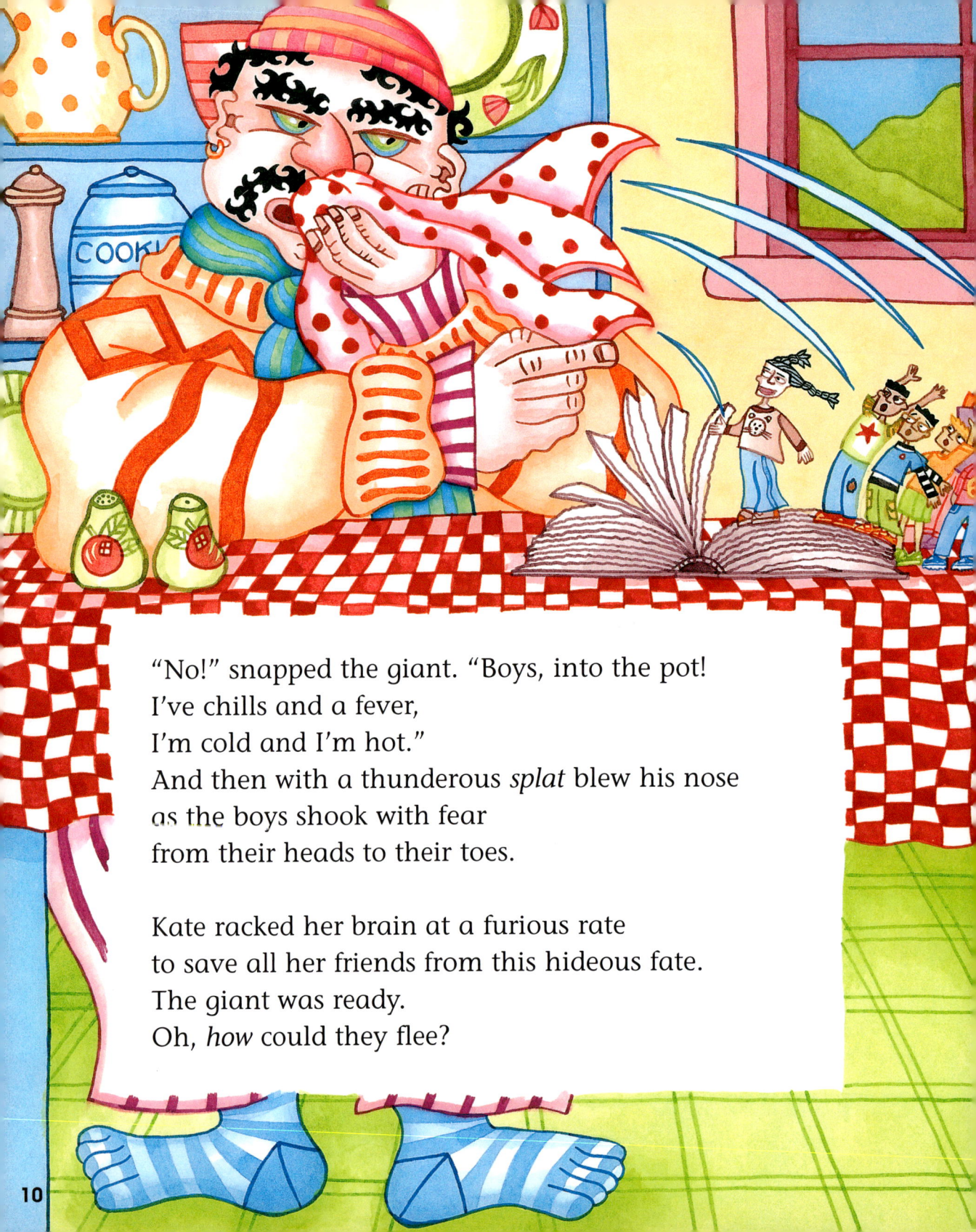

"No!" snapped the giant. "Boys, into the pot!
I've chills and a fever,
I'm cold and I'm hot."
And then with a thunderous *splat* blew his nose
as the boys shook with fear
from their heads to their toes.

Kate racked her brain at a furious rate
to save all her friends from this hideous fate.
The giant was ready.
Oh, *how* could they flee?

Their ten rubber running shoes—
that was the key!

Just as the giant came closer to scoop
the lads for his horrid medicinal soup,
Kate gave a signal, the tiniest look.
The boys understood. They leapt to the book
and started a dance, half a shuffle, half-run,
and jogged back and forth
on page seventy-one.
Up the page, down the page
sidestep, repeat—

til most
of each word
was erased
by their feet.

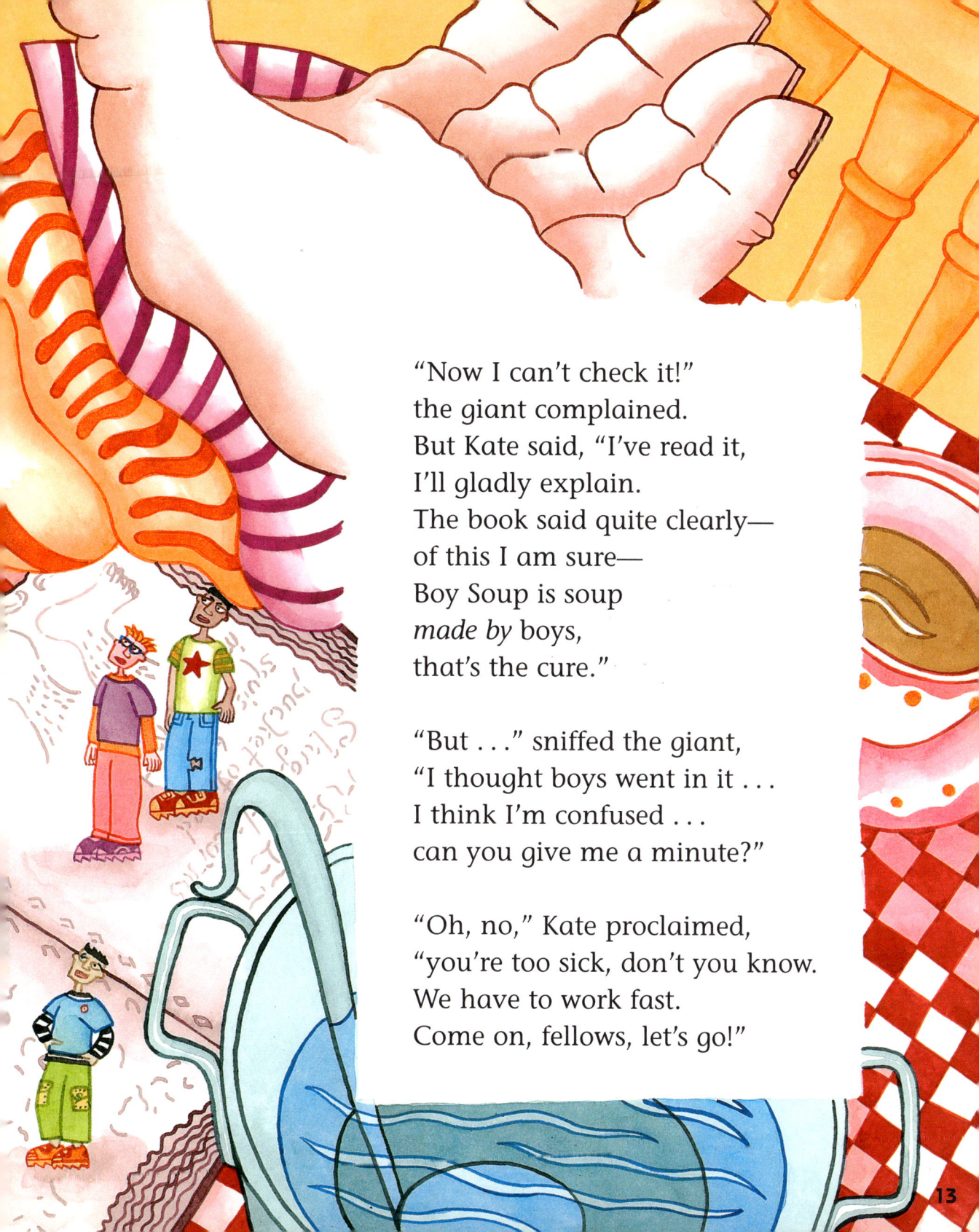

"Now I can't check it!"
the giant complained.
But Kate said, "I've read it,
I'll gladly explain.
The book said quite clearly—
of this I am sure—
Boy Soup is soup
made by boys,
that's the cure."

"But . . ." sniffed the giant,
"I thought boys went in it . . .
I think I'm confused . . .
can you give me a minute?"

"Oh, no," Kate proclaimed,
"you're too sick, don't you know.
We have to work fast.
Come on, fellows, let's go!"

The boys cooked the carrots
the boys boiled the peas
then seasoned the soup with
a handful of fleas.

They put in
some mud
and some thick, yellow glue
and a generous dollop of dandruff shampoo.

Kate poured in
pepper
and red-hot sauce,
rotten bananas,
and candy floss,
sour green pickles,
and beans in the can
all simmered together as part of the plan.

And oh, the aroma!
Like skunk in a pot.

Kate smiled her sweetest
and served it up hot.

In between snuffles, the giant took sips
from a spoon trembling close
to his great hairy lips.

He scowled in suspicion but took one more taste,
with a huge doughy tongue
much the color of paste—

Then tipped the whole potful of soup down his throat
. . . sat back . . .
and sighed—
til he started to bloat!
With the pepper, the mud, and the pickles combined,
the giant let out a most terrible whine—

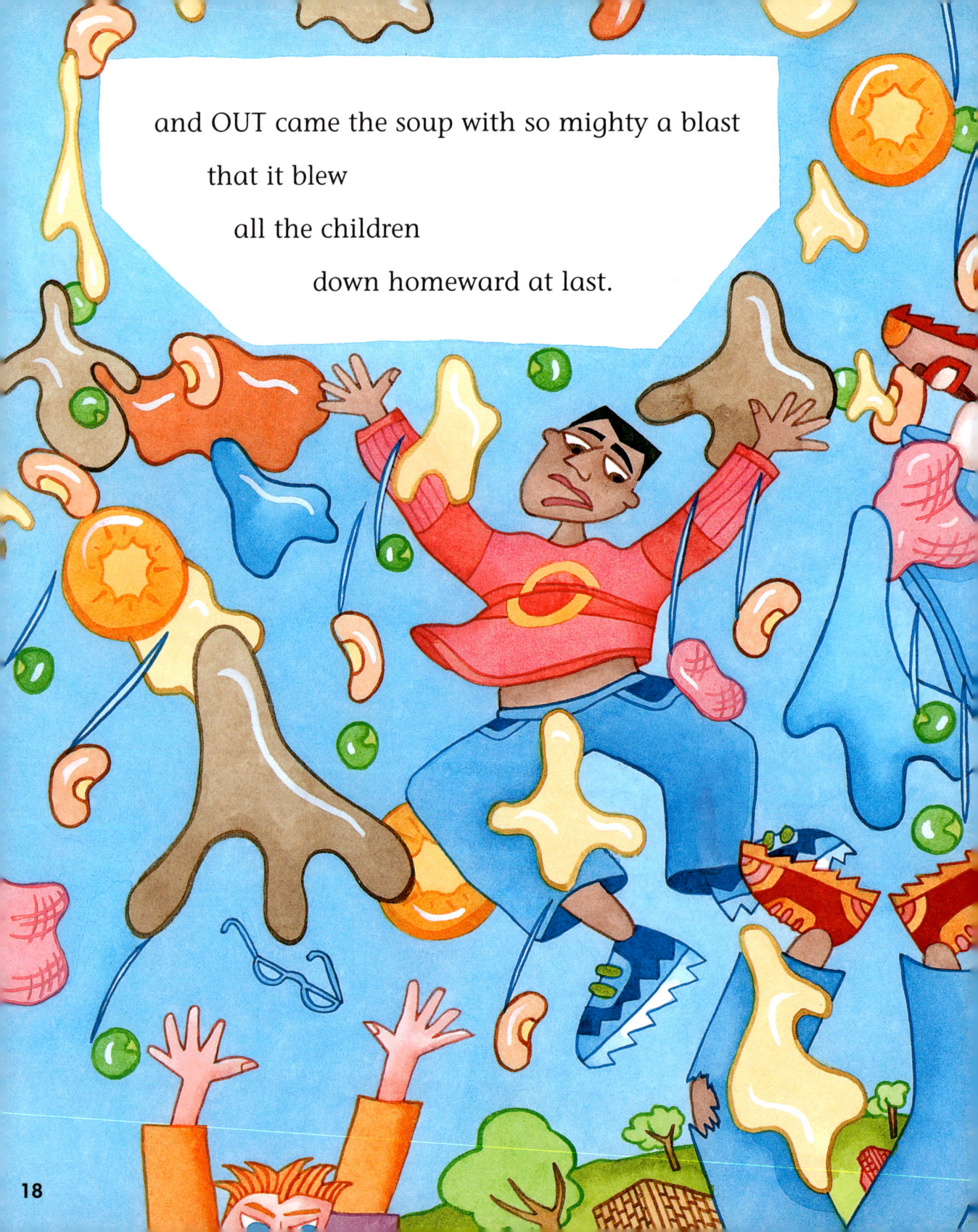

and OUT came the soup with so mighty a blast
that it blew
all the children
down homeward at last.

Kate and the fellows
were dented, but sound,
when they landed back home
on familiar ground . . .

They needed new sneakers,
and something to do
to get over the horrible shock
they'd been through.

The giant was not
who they wanted to feed,
but they *had* liked the cooking,
with Kate in the lead.

They opened "Boys' Restaurant"
as a group—
and served almost everything
but Boy Soup.

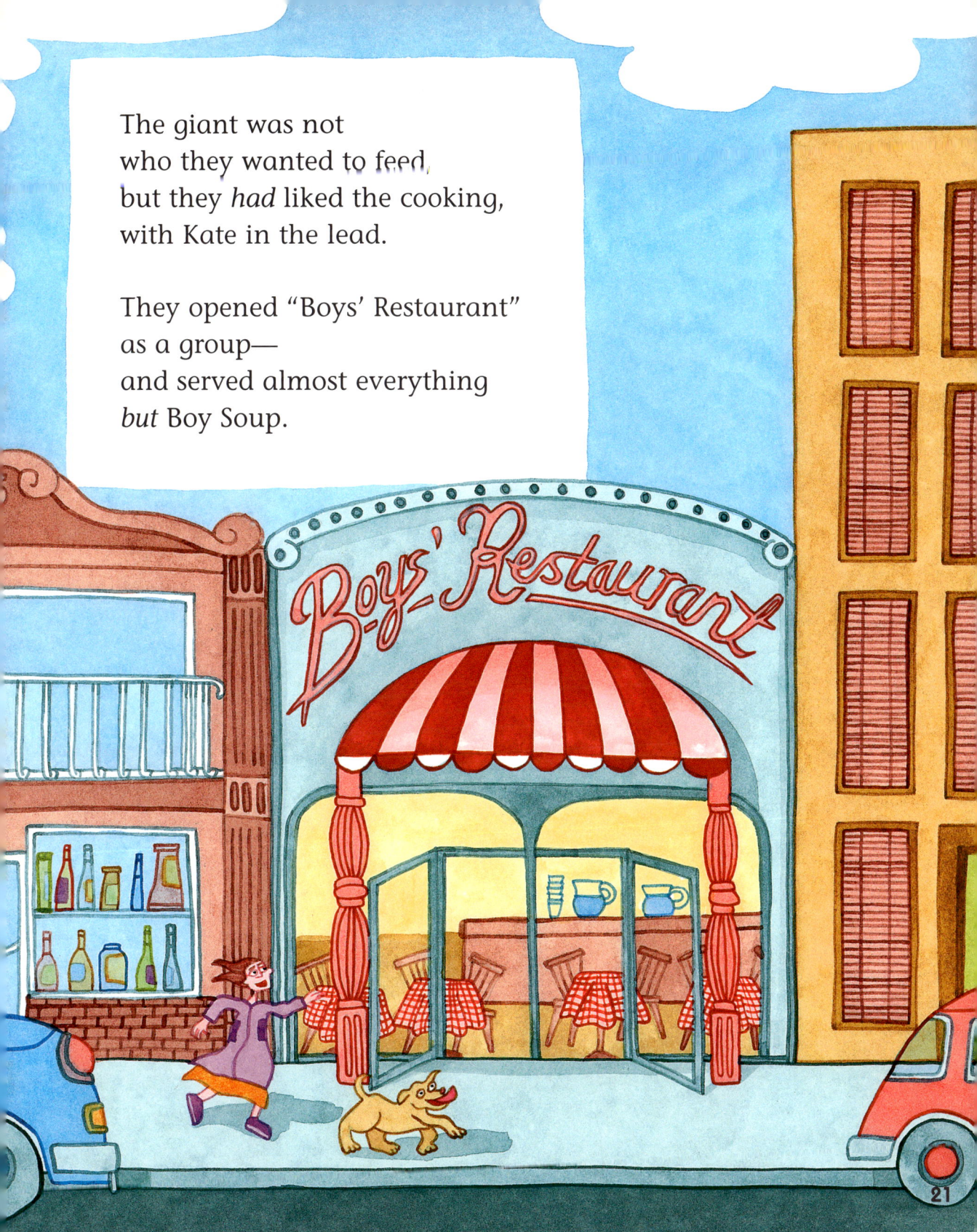

One day at the restaurant, delivery came of an extra-large envelope bearing Kate's name. The giant had written: